Beaded Ornaments TO KNIT

Whether you've just started knitting or been knitting for years, you'll love fashioning these sparkling orbs! Each of the twelve designs cradles a clear glass ornament inside, and each knitted creation is highlighted by dozens of beads. Use yarn enhanced with a metallic thread to make your knitted orbs glow with reflected light. Display them near a window, heap them in bowls or vases, or hang them on ornament stands. These decorator items are beautiful year-round, and they make wonderful gifts!

LEISURE ARTS, INC.
LITTLE ROCK, ARKANSAS

Christmas Joy

INTERMEDIATE

MATERIALS

Light Weight Yarn
25 yards (23 meters)
4 Double pointed needles, size 5 (3.75 mm) **or** size needed for gauge
192 Glass beads (4 mm round beads, size 6 seed beads, **or** E beads)
2 5/8" (6.5 cm) Diameter round glass ornament
Split-ring marker
Tapestry needle

GAUGE: In Stockinette Stitch,
13 sts and 18 rows = 2" (5 cm)

BODY

String 192 beads onto the yarn ***(see Stringing Beads, page 23)***.

Leaving a 12" (30.5 cm) tail, cast on 6 sts.

Row 1 (Right side)**:** K1, increase 5 times ***(see Knit Increase, page 23)***: 11 sts.

Row 2: Purl across.

Row 3: K1, increase 10 times: 21 sts.

Row 4: Purl across.

Row 5: K3, increase 15 times, K3: 36 sts.

Begin working in rounds on **three** double pointed needles ***(see Using Double Pointed Needles, page 23);*** place marker ***(see Markers, page 22):*** 12 sts per needle.

Rnd 1: Knit around.

Rnd 2: (K6, slip 1 bead) around.

Rnd 3: K1, slip 1 bead, K4, slip 1 bead, ★ K2, slip1 bead, K4, slip 1 bead; repeat from ★ around to last st, K1.

Rnd 4: (K2, slip 1 bead) twice, ★ K4, slip 1 bead, K2, slip 1 bead; repeat from ★ around to last 2 sts, K2.

Rnd 5: K3, slip 1 bead, (K6, slip 1 bead) around to last 3 sts, K3.

Rnd 6: (K2, slip 1 bead) twice, ★ K4, slip 1 bead, K2, slip 1 bead; repeat from ★ around to last 2 sts, K2.

Rnd 7: K1, slip 1 bead, K4, slip 1 bead, ★ K2, slip 1 bead, K4, slip 1 bead; repeat from ★ around to last st, K1.

Rnds 8-10: Repeat Rnds 2-4.

Rnd 11: (K3, slip 1 bead) around.

Rnds 12 and 13: Repeat Rnds 6 and 7.

Rnds 14-20: Repeat Rnds 2-7 once, then repeat Rnd 2 once **more**.

Rnds 21 and 22: Knit around.

See **Finishing**, page 23, to complete your ornament.

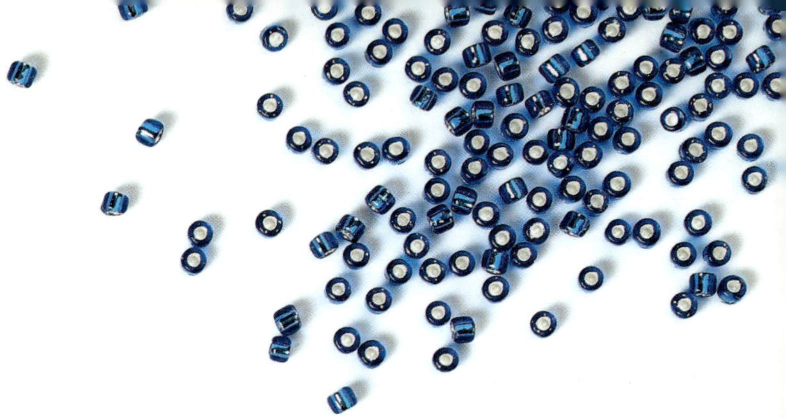

Windowpanes

INTERMEDIATE

MATERIALS

Light Weight Yarn (LIGHT 3)
- 25 yards (23 meters)

4 Double pointed needles, size 5 (3.75 mm)
- **or** size needed for gauge

156 Glass beads (4 mm round beads,
- size 6 seed beads, **or** E beads)

2⅝" (6.5 cm) Diameter round glass ornament

Split-ring marker

Tapestry needle

GAUGE: In Stockinette Stitch, 13 sts and 18 rows = 2" (5 cm).

BODY

String 156 beads onto the yarn ***(see Stringing Beads, page 23)***.

Leaving a 12" (30.5 cm) tail, cast on 6 sts.

Row 1 (Right side)**:** K1, increase 5 times ***(see Knit Increase, page 23)***: 11 sts.

Row 2: Purl across.

Row 3: K1, increase 10 times: 21 sts.

Row 4: Purl across.

Row 5: K3, increase 15 times, K3: 36 sts.

Begin working in rounds on **three** double pointed needles ***(see Using Double Pointed Needles, page 23);*** place marker ***(see Markers, page 22):*** 12 sts per needle.

Rnd 1: Knit around.

Rnd 2: (K6, slip 1 bead) around.

Rnd 3: K1, slip 1 bead, K4, slip 1 bead, ★ K2, slip 1 bead, K4, slip 1 bead; repeat from ★ around to last st, K1.

Instructions continued on page 8.

Rnd 4: (K2, slip 1 bead) twice, ★ K4, slip 1 bead, K2, slip 1 bead; repeat from ★ around to last 2 sts, K2.

Rnd 5: K3, slip 1 bead, (K6, slip 1 bead) around to last 3 sts, K3.

Rnd 6: Knit around.

Rnd 7: (K3, slip 1 bead) around.

Rnd 8: Knit around.

Rnd 9: (K3, slip 1 bead) around.

Rnd 10: K1, slip 1 bead, K4, slip 1 bead, ★ K2, slip 1 bead, K4, slip 1 bead; repeat from ★ around to last st, K1.

Rnd 11: (K3, slip 1 bead) around.

Rnds 12 and 13: Repeat Rnds 10 and 11.

Rnd 14: Knit around.

Rnds 15 and 16: Repeat Rnds 7 and 8.

Rnd 17: Repeat Rnd 5.

Rnd 18: Repeat Rnd 4.

Rnd 19: Repeat Rnd 3.

Rnd 20: Repeat Rnd 2.

Rnds 21 and 22: Knit around.

See **Finishing**, page 23, to complete your ornament.

Fleur De Lis

INTERMEDIATE

MATERIALS

Light Weight Yarn (LIGHT 3)
- 25 yards (23 meters)

4 Double pointed needles, size 5 (3.75 mm) **or** size needed for gauge

162 Glass beads (4 mm round beads, size 6 seed beads, **or** E beads)

2⁵/₈" (6.5 cm) Diameter round glass ornament

Split-ring marker

Tapestry needle

GAUGE: In Stockinette Stitch,
13 sts and 18 rows = 2" (5 cm)

BODY

String 162 beads onto the yarn ***(see Stringing Beads, page 23)***.

Leaving a 12" (30.5 cm) tail, cast on 6 sts.

Row 1 (Right side)**:** K1, increase 5 times ***(see Knit Increase, page 23)***: 11 sts.

Row 2: Purl across.

Row 3: K1, increase 10 times: 21 sts.

Row 4: Purl across.

Row 5: K3, increase 15 times, K3: 36 sts.

Begin working in rounds on **three** double pointed needles ***(see Using Double Pointed Needles, page 23);*** place marker ***(see Markers, page 22):*** 12 sts per needle.

Rnd 1: Knit around.

Rnd 2: (K4, slip 1 bead) around.

Rnd 3: K2, slip 1 bead, (K4, slip 1 bead) around to last 2 sts, K2.

Rnd 4: (K4, slip 1 bead) around.

Rnds 5 and 6: Knit around.

Rnd 7: K2, slip 1 bead, (K4, slip 1 bead) around to last 2 sts, K2.

Rnd 8: K2, slip 2 beads, (K4, slip 2 beads) around to last 2 sts, K2.

Rnd 9: K2, slip 1 bead, (K4, slip 1 bead) around to last 2 sts, K2.

Rnd 10: (K4, slip 1 bead) around.

Rnd 11: (K4, slip 2 beads) around.

Rnd 12: (K4, slip 1 bead) around.

Rnds 13-15: Repeat Rnds 7-9.

Rnds 16 and 17: Knit around.

Rnds 18-20: Repeat Rnds 2-4.

Rnds 21 and 22: Knit around.

See **Finishing**, page 23, to complete your ornament.

Ups and Downs

INTERMEDIATE

MATERIALS
Light Weight Yarn (LIGHT 3)
25 yards (23 meters)
4 Double pointed needles, size 5 (3.75 mm) **or** size needed for gauge
144 Glass beads (4 mm round beads, size 6 seed beads, **or** E beads)
$2\frac{5}{8}$" (6.5 cm) Diameter round glass ornament
Split-ring marker
Tapestry needle

GAUGE: In Stockinette Stitch,
13 sts and 18 rows = 2" (5 cm)

BODY

String 144 beads onto the yarn ***(see Stringing Beads, page 23)***.

Leaving a 12" (30.5 cm) tail, cast on 6 sts.

Row 1 (Right side)**:** K1, increase 5 times ***(see Knit Increase, page 23)***: 11 sts.

Row 2: Purl across.

Row 3: K1, increase 10 times: 21 sts.

Row 4: Purl across.

Row 5: K3, increase 15 times, K3: 36 sts.

Begin working in rounds on **three** double pointed needles ***(see Using Double Pointed Needles, page 23);*** place marker ***(see Markers, page 22):*** 12 sts per needle.

Rnd 1: Knit around.

Rnd 2: (K6, slip 1 bead) around.

Rnds 3-6: Repeat Rnds 1 and 2 twice.

Rnd 7: K3, slip 1 bead, (K6, slip 1 bead) around to last 3 sts, K3.

Rnd 8: ★ K3, slip 2 beads, K3, slip 1 bead; repeat from ★ around.

Rnd 9: K3, slip 3 beads, (K6, slip 3 beads) around to last 3 sts, K3.

Rnd 10: (K3, slip 1 bead) around.

Rnd 11: Knit around.

Rnd 12: (K3, slip 1 bead) around.

Rnd 13: (K6, slip 3 beads) around.

Rnd 14: ★ K3, slip 1 bead, K3, slip 2 beads; repeat from ★ around.

Rnd 15: (K6, slip 1 bead) around.

Rnd 16: K3, slip 1 bead, (K6, slip 1 bead) around to last 3 sts, K3.

Rnd 17: Knit around.

Rnds 18-21: Repeat Rnds 16 and 17 twice.

Rnd 22: Knit around.

See **Finishing**, page 23, to complete your ornament.

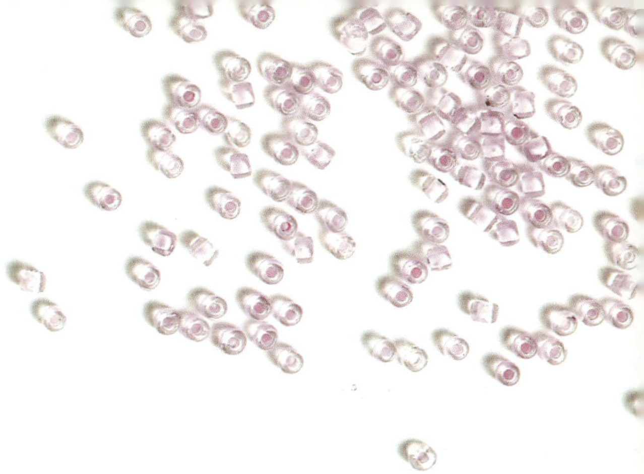

Zig Zag

INTERMEDIATE

MATERIALS
Light Weight Yarn (LIGHT 3)
25 yards (23 meters)
4 Double pointed needles,
size 5 (3.75 mm)
or size needed for gauge
114 Glass beads (4 mm round beads,
size 6 seed beads, **or** E beads)
2⅝" (6.5 cm) Diameter round glass ornament
Split-ring marker
Tapestry needle

GAUGE: In Stockinette Stitch,
13 sts and 18 rows = 2" (5 cm)

BODY

String 114 beads onto the yarn ***(see Stringing Beads, page 23)***.

Leaving a 12" (30.5 cm) tail, cast on 6 sts.

Row 1 (Right side)**:** K1, increase 5 times ***(see Knit Increase, page 23)***: 11 sts.

Row 2: Purl across.

Row 3: K1, increase 10 times: 21 sts.

Row 4: Purl across.

Row 5: K3, increase 15 times, K3: 36 sts.

Instructions continued on page 12.

Begin working in rounds on **three** double pointed needles ***(see Using Double Pointed Needles, page 23);*** place marker ***(see Markers, page 22):*** 12 sts per needle.

Rnd 1: Knit around.

Rnd 2: (K6, slip 1 bead) around.

Rnd 3: K5, slip 1 bead, (K6, slip 1 bead) around to last st, K1.

Rnd 4: K4, slip 1 bead, (K6, slip 1 bead) around to last 2 sts, K2.

Rnd 5: K3, slip 1 bead, (K6, slip 1 bead) around to last, 3 sts, K3.

Rnd 6: K4, slip 1 bead, (K6, slip 1 bead) around to last 2 sts, K2.

Rnd 7: K5, slip 1 bead, (K6, slip 1 bead) around to last st, K1.

Rnds 8-20: Repeat Rnds 2-7 twice, then Rnd 2 once **more**.

Rnds 21 and 22: Knit around.

See **Finishing**, page 23, to complete your ornament.

Cross

INTERMEDIATE

MATERIALS

LIGHT 3

- Light Weight Yarn
  - 25 yards (23 meters)
- 4 Double pointed needles,
  - size 5 (3.75 mm) **or** size needed for gauge
- 104 Glass beads (4 mm round beads,
  - size 6 seed beads, **or** E beads)
- 2⅝" (6.5 cm) Diameter round glass ornament
- Split-ring marker
- Tapestry needle

GAUGE: In Stockinette Stitch,
13 sts and 18 rows = 2" (5 cm)

BODY

String 104 beads onto the yarn ***(see Stringing Beads, page 23)***.

Leaving a 12" (30.5 cm) tail, cast on 6 sts.

Row 1 (Right side)**:** K1, increase 5 times ***(see Knit Increase, page 23)***: 11 sts.

Row 2: Purl across.

Row 3: K1, increase 10 times: 21 sts.

Row 4: Purl across.

Row 5: K3, increase 15 times, K3: 36 sts.

Begin working in rounds on **three** double pointed needles ***(see Using Double Pointed Needles, page 23);*** place marker ***(see Markers, page 22):*** 12 sts per needle.

Rnds 1-3: Knit around.

Rnd 4: K4, slip 1 bead, K1, slip 1 bead, ★ K8, slip 1 bead, K1, slip 1 bead; repeat from ★ 2 times **more**, K4.

Rnd 5: Knit around.

Rnds 6-13: Repeat Rnds 4 and 5, 4 times.

Rnd 14: K2, slip 1 bead, (K1, slip 1 bead) 5 times, ★ K4, slip 1 bead, (K1, slip 1 bead) 5 times; repeat from ★ 2 times **more**, K2.

Rnd 15: Knit around.

Rnd 16: Repeat Rnd 14.

Rnd 17: Knit around.

Rnd 18: K4, slip 1 bead, K1, slip 1 bead, ★ K8, slip 1 bead, K1, slip 1 bead; repeat from ★ around to last 4 sts, K4.

Rnds 19 and 20: Repeat Rnds 17 and 18.

Rnds 21-24: Knit around.

See **Finishing**, page 23, to complete your ornament.

Diamond

INTERMEDIATE

MATERIALS

Light Weight Yarn
  25 yards (23 meters)
4 Double pointed needles, size 5 (3.75 mm)
  or size needed for gauge
162 Glass beads (4 mm round beads,
  size 6 seed beads, **or** E beads)
$2^5/_8$" (6.5 cm) Diameter round glass ornament
Split-ring marker
Tapestry needle

GAUGE: In Stockinette Stitch,
13 sts and 18 rows = 2" (5 cm)

BODY

String 162 beads onto the yarn ***(see Stringing Beads, page 23)***.

Leaving a 12" (30.5 cm) tail, cast on 6 sts.

Row 1 (Right side)**:** K1, increase 5 times ***(see Knit Increase, page 23)***: 11 sts.

Row 2: Purl across.

Row 3: K1, increase 10 times: 21 sts.

Row 4: Purl across.

Row 5: K3, increase 15 times, K3: 36 sts.

Begin working in rounds on **three** double pointed needles ***(see Using Double Pointed Needles, page 23);*** place marker ***(see Markers, page 22):*** 12 sts per needle.

Rnds 1-4: Knit around.

Rnd 5: (K6, slip 1 bead) around.

Rnds 6 and 7: Knit around.

Rnd 8: (K6, slip 1 bead) around.

Rnd 9: (K6, slip 2 beads) around.

Rnd 10: (K6, slip 3 beads) around.

Rnd 11: (K6, slip 4 beads) around.

Rnd 12: (K6, slip 5 beads) around.

Rnd 13: (K6, slip 4 beads) around.

Rnd 14: (K6, slip 3 beads) around.

Rnd 15: (K6, slip 2 beads) around.

Rnd 16: (K6, slip 1 bead) around.

Rnds 17 and 18: Knit around.

Rnd 19: (K6, slip 1 bead) around.

Rnds 20-22: Knit around.

See **Finishing**, page 23, to complete your ornament.

Vertical

INTERMEDIATE

MATERIALS LIGHT 3

Light Weight Yarn
25 yards (23 meters)
4 Double pointed needles,
size 5 (3.75 mm)
or size needed for gauge
180 Glass beads (4 mm round beads,
size 6 seed beads, **or** E beads)
2 5/8" (6.5 cm) Diameter round glass ornament
Split-ring marker
Tapestry needle

GAUGE: In Stockinette Stitch,
13 sts and 18 rows = 2" (5 cm)

BODY

String 180 beads onto the yarn ***(see Stringing Beads, page 23)***.

Leaving a 12" (30.5 cm) tail, cast on 6 sts.

Row 1 (Right side)**:** K1, increase 5 times ***(see Knit Increase, page 23)***: 11 sts.

Row 2: Purl across.

Row 3: K1, increase 10 times: 21 sts.

Row 4: Purl across.

Row 5: K3, increase 15 times, K3: 36 sts.

Begin working in rounds on **three** double pointed needles ***(see Using Double Pointed Needles, page 23);*** place marker ***(see Markers, page 22):*** 12 sts per needle.

Rnd 1: Knit around.

Rnds 2-21: (K4, slip 1 bead) around.

Rnds 22 and 23: Knit around.

See **Finishing**, page 23, to complete your ornament.

Holiday Greetings

■■■□ INTERMEDIATE

MATERIALS

Light Weight Yarn (3 LIGHT)
  25 yards (23 meters)
4 Double pointed needles, size 5 (3.75 mm)
  or size needed for gauge
164 Glass beads (4 mm round beads,
  size 6 seed beads, **or** E beads)
2⅝" (6.5 cm) Diameter round glass ornament
Split-ring marker
Tapestry needle

GAUGE: In Stockinette Stitch,
13 sts and 18 rows = 2" (5 cm)

BODY

String 164 beads onto the yarn ***(see Stringing Beads, page 23)***.

Leaving a 12" (30.5 cm) tail, cast on 6 sts.

Row 1 (Right side)**:** K1, increase 5 times ***(see Knit Increase, page 23)***: 11 sts.

Row 2: Purl across.

Row 3: K1, increase 10 times: 21 sts.

Row 4: Purl across.

Row 5: K3, increase 15 times, K3: 36 sts.

Begin working in rounds on **three** double pointed needles ***(see Using Double Pointed Needles, page 23);*** place marker ***(see Markers, page 22):*** 12 sts per needle.

Rnd 1: Knit around.

Rnd 2: K4, slip 1 bead, (K9, slip 1 bead) 3 times, K5.

Rnd 3: Knit around.

Rnd 4: K3, slip 1 bead, (K1, slip bead) twice ★ K7, slip 1 bead, (K1, slip 1 bead) twice; repeat from ★ 2 times **more**, K4.

Rnd 5: Knit around.

Rnd 6: K2, slip 1 bead, (K1, slip 1 bead) 4 times, ★ K5, slip 1 bead, (K1, slip 1 bead) 4 times; repeat from ★ 2 times **more**, K3.

Rnd 7: Knit around.

Rnd 8: (K1, slip 1 bead) 7 times, ★ K3, slip 1 bead, (K1, slip 1 bead) 6 times; repeat from ★ 2 times **more**, K2.

Rnd 9: Knit around.

Rnd 10: (K1, slip 1 bead) around.

Rnds 11 and 12: Repeat Rnds 7 an

Rnds 13 and 14: Repeat Rnds 5 and 6.

Rnds 15 and 16: Repeat Rnds 3 and 4.

Rnds 17 and 18: Repeat Rnds 1 and 2.

Rnds 19 and 20: Knit around.

See **Finishing**, page 23, to complete your ornament.

Double Diamonds

INTERMEDIATE

MATERIALS

LIGHT 3

Light Weight Yarn
25 yards (23 meters)
4 Double pointed needles, size 5 (3.75 mm) **or** size needed for gauge
120 Glass beads (4 mm round beads, size 6 seed beads, **or** E beads)
2⁵/₈" (6.5 cm) Diameter round glass ornament
Split-ring marker
Tapestry needle

GAUGE: In Stockinette Stitch,
13 sts and 18 rows = 2" (5 cm)

BODY

String 120 beads onto the yarn ***(see Stringing Beads, page 23)***.

Leaving a 12" (30.5 cm) tail, cast on 6 sts.

Row 1 (Right side)**:** K1, increase 5 times ***(see Knit Increase, page 23)***: 11 sts.

Row 2: Purl across.

Row 3: K1, increase 10 times: 21 sts.

Row 4: Purl across.

Row 5: K3, increase 15 times, K3: 36 sts.

Instructions continued on page 18.

Begin working in rounds on **three** double pointed needles ***(see Using Double Pointed Needles, page 23);*** place marker ***(see Markers, page 22):*** 12 sts per needle.

Rnds 1-3: Knit around.

Rnd 4: K1, slip 1 bead, K 10, slip 1 bead, ★ K2, slip 1 bead, K 10, slip 1 bead; repeat from ★ once **more**, K1.

Rnd 5: (K 12, slip 1 bead) around.

Rnd 6: Knit around.

Rnd 7: K6, slip 1 bead, (K 12, slip 1 bead) twice, K6.

Rnd 8: K5, slip 1 bead, K2, slip 1 bead, ★ K 10, slip 1 bead, K2, slip 1 bead; repeat from ★ once **more**, K5.

Rnd 9: (K4, slip 1 bead) twice, ★ K8, slip 1 bead, K4, slip 1 bead; repeat from ★ once **more**, K4.

Rnd 10: K3, slip 1 bead, (K6, slip 1 bead) around to last 3 sts, K3.

Rnd 11: K2, slip 1 bead, (K4, slip 1 bead) around to last 2 sts, K2.

Rnd 12: K1, slip 1 bead, K4, slip 1 bead, ★ K2, slip 1 bead, K4, slip 1 bead; repeat from ★ around to last st, K1.

Rnd 13: (K2, slip 1 bead) around.

Rnd 14: Repeat Rnd 12.

Rnd 15: Repeat Rnd 11.

Rnd 16: Repeat Rnd 10.

Rnd 17: Repeat Rnd 9.

Rnd 18: Repeat Rnd 8.

Rnd 19: Repeat Rnd 7.

Rnd 20: Knit around.

Rnd 21: (K 12, slip 1 bead) around.

Rnd 22: Repeat Rnd 4.

Rnds 23 and 24: Knit around.

See **Finishing**, page 23, to complete your ornament.

Diamond Trio

INTERMEDIATE

MATERIALS

Light Weight Yarn (LIGHT 3)
  25 yards (23 meters)
4 Double pointed needles, size 5 (3.75 mm)
  or size needed for gauge
108 Glass beads (4 mm round beads,
  size 6 seed beads, **or** E beads)
$2^{5}/_{8}$" (6.5 cm) Diameter round glass ornament
Split-ring marker
Tapestry needle

GAUGE: In Stockinette Stitch,
13 sts and 18 rows = 2" (5 cm)

BODY

String 108 beads onto the yarn ***(see Stringing Beads, page 23)***.

Leaving a 12" (30.5 cm) tail, cast on 6 sts.

Row 1 (Right side)**:** K1, increase 5 times ***(see Knit Increase, page 23)***: 11 sts.

Row 2: Purl across.

Row 3: K1, increase 10 times: 21 sts.

Row 4: Purl across.

Row 5: K3, increase 15 times, K3: 36 sts.

Begin working in rounds on **three** double pointed needles ***(see Using Double Pointed Needles, page 23);*** place marker ***(see Markers, page 22):*** 12 sts per needle.

Rnd 1: Knit around.

Rnd 2: (K6, slip 1 bead) around.

Rnd 3: K2, slip 1 bead, K8, slip 1 bead, ★ K4, slip 1 bead, K8, slip 1 bead; repeat from ★ once **more**, K2.

Rnd 4: (K4, slip 1 bead) twice, ★ K8, slip 1 bead, K4, slip 1 bead; repeat from ★ once **more**, K4.

Rnd 5: (K 12, slip 1 bead) around.

Rnd 6: K2, slip 1 bead, K8, slip 1 bead, ★ K4, slip 1 bead, K8, slip 1 bead; repeat from ★ once **more**, K2.

Instructions continued on page 20.

Rnd 7: Knit around.

Rnd 8: (K6, slip 1 bead) around.

Rnd 9: K5, slip 1 bead, K2, slip 1 bead, ★ K 10, slip 1 bead, K2, slip 1 bead; repeat from ★ once **more**, K5.

Rnd 10: K4, slip 1 bead, (K2, slip 1 bead) twice, ★ K8, slip 1 bead, (K2, slip 1 bead) twice; repeat from ★ once **more**, K4.

Rnd 11: K3, slip 1 bead, (K2, slip 1 bead) 3 times, ★ K6, slip 1 bead, (K2, slip 1 bead) 3 times; repeat from ★ once **more**, K3.

Rnd 12: Repeat Rnd 10.

Rnd 13: Repeat Rnd 9.

Rnd 14: (K6, slip 1 bead) around.

Rnd 15: Knit around.

Rnd 16: Repeat Rnd 6.

Rnd 17: (K 12, slip 1 bead) around.

Rnd 18: Repeat Rnd 4.

Rnd 19: Repeat Rnd 3.

Rnd 20: (K6, slip 1 bead) around.

Rnds 21 and 22: Knit around.

See **Finishing**, page 23, to complete your ornament.

Hearts

INTERMEDIATE

MATERIALS

LIGHT 3

Light Weight Yarn
25 yards (23 meters)
4 Double pointed needles, size 5 (3.75 mm) **or** size needed for gauge
147 Glass beads (4 mm round beads, size 6 seed beads, **or** E beads)
$2^5/_8$" (6.5 cm) Diameter round glass ornament
Split-ring marker
Tapestry needle

GAUGE: In Stockinette Stitch,
13 sts and 18 rows = 2" (5 cm)

BODY

String 147 beads onto the yarn ***(see Stringing Beads, page 23)***.

Leaving a 12" (30.5 cm) tail, cast on 6 sts.

Row 1 (Right side)**:** K1, increase 5 times ***(see Knit Increase, page 23)***: 11 sts.

Row 2: Purl across.

Row 3: K1, increase 10 times: 21 sts.

Row 4: Purl across.

Row 5: K2, increase 18 times, K1: 39 sts.

Begin working in rounds on **three** double pointed needles ***(see Using Double Pointed Needles, page 23);*** place marker ***(see Markers, page 22):*** 12 sts per needle.

Rnds 1-4: Knit around.

Rnd 5: K7, slip 1 bead, (K 13, slip 1 bead) twice, K6.

Rnd 6: K6, slip 1 bead, K2, slip 1 bead, ★ K 11, slip 1 bead, K2, slip 1 bead; repeat from ★ once **more**, K5.

Rnd 7: K5, slip 1 bead, (K2, slip 1 bead) twice, ★ K9, slip 1 bead, (K2, slip 1 bead) twice; repeat from ★ once **more**, K4.

Rnd 8: K4, slip 1 bead, (K2, slip 1 bead) 3 times, ★ K7, slip 1 bead, (K2, slip 1 bead) 3 times; repeat from ★ once **more**, K3.

Rnd 9: K3, slip 1 bead, (K2, slip 1 bead) 4 times, ★ K5, slip 1 bead, (K2, slip 1 bead) 4 times; repeat from ★ once **more**, K2.

Rnd 10: K2, slip 1 bead, (K2, slip 1 bead) 5 times, ★ K3, slip 1 bead, (K2, slip 1 bead) 5 times; repeat from ★ once **more**, K1.

Rnds 11-14: Repeat Rnds 9 and 10 twice.

Rnd 15: K3, slip 1 bead, K2, slip 1 bead, K4, slip 1 bead, K2, slip 1 bead, ★ K5, slip 1 bead, K2, slip 1 bead, K4, slip 1 bead, K2 slip 1 bead; repeat from ★ once **more**, K2.

Rnd 16: K4, slip 1 bead, K6, slip 1 bead, ★ K7, slip 1 bead, K6, slip 1 bead; repeat from ★ once **more**, K3.

Rnds 17-21: Knit around.

See **Finishing**, page 23, to complete your ornament.

General Instructions

ABBREVIATIONS

cm	centimeters
K	Knit
mm	millimeters
Rnd(s)	Round(s)
st(s)	stitch(es)

★ — work instructions following ★ as many **more** times as indicated in addition to the first time.

( ) — work enclosed instructions **as many** times as specified by the number immediatley following **or** work all enclosed instructions in stitch **or** space indicated or contains explanatory remarks.

colon (:) — the number(s) given after a colon at the end of a row or round denote(s) the number of stitches or spaces you should have on that row or round.

GAUGE

Exact gauge is **essential** for proper size. Needle size given in instructions is merely a guide and should never be used without first making a sample swatch approximately 2" (5 cm) square in the stitch, yarn, and needle specified. Then measure it, counting your stitches and rows or rounds carefully. If your swatch is larger or smaller than specified, **make another, changing needle size to get the correct gauge**. Keep trying until you find the size needle that will give you the specified gauge.

MARKERS

As a convenience to you, we have used markers to help distinguish the beginning of a round. Place markers as instructed.

When using double pointed needles and marking the beginning of a round, a split-ring marker is placed around the first stitch to prevent the marker from slipping off the needle. When you reach the marker, move it to the new stitch after it has been made. Remove it when it is no longer needed.

KNIT TERMINOLOGY		
UNITED STATES		**INTERNATIONAL**
gauge	=	tension
bind off	=	cast off
yarn over (YO)	=	yarn forward (yfwd) **or** yarn around needle (yrn)

Yarn Weight Symbol & Names	SUPER FINE 1	FINE 2	LIGHT 3	MEDIUM 4	BULKY 5	SUPER BULKY 6
Type of Yarns in Category	Sock, Fingering Baby	Sport, Baby	DK, Light Worsted	Worsted, Afghan, Aran	Chunky, Craft, Rug	Bulky, Roving
Knit Gauge Ranges in Stockinette St to 4" (10 cm)	27-32 sts	23-26 sts	21-24 sts	16-20 sts	12-15 sts	6-11 sts
Advised Needle Size Range	1-3	3-5	5-7	7-9	9-11	11 and larger

KNITTING NEEDLES																
U.S.	0	1	2	3	4	5	6	7	8	9	10	10½	11	13	15	17
U.K.	13	12	11	10	9	8	7	6	5	4	3	2	1	00	000	---
Metric - mm	2	2.25	2.75	3.25	3.5	3.75	4	4.5	5	5.5	6	6.5	8	9	10	12.75

BEGINNER	Projects for first-time knitters using basic knit and purl stitches. Minimal shaping.
EASY	Projects using basic stitches, repetitive stitch patterns, simple color changes, and simple shaping and finishing.
INTERMEDIATE	Projects with a variety of stitches, such as basic cables and lace, simple intarsia, double-pointed needles and knitting in the round needle techniques, mid-level shaping and finishing.
EXPERIENCED	Projects using advanced techniques and stitches, such as short rows, fair isle, more intricate intarsia, cables, lace patterns, and numerous color changes.

STRINGING BEADS

To string the beads, make a harness using a sewing needle and thread. Insert a 4" (10 cm) length of thread through the eye of the needle. Tie a square knot in the thread (left over right and right over left). Holding both loose ends of the thread, pull the circle open until the knot is secured. Loop the yarn through the harness ***(Fig. 1)***.

Fig. 1

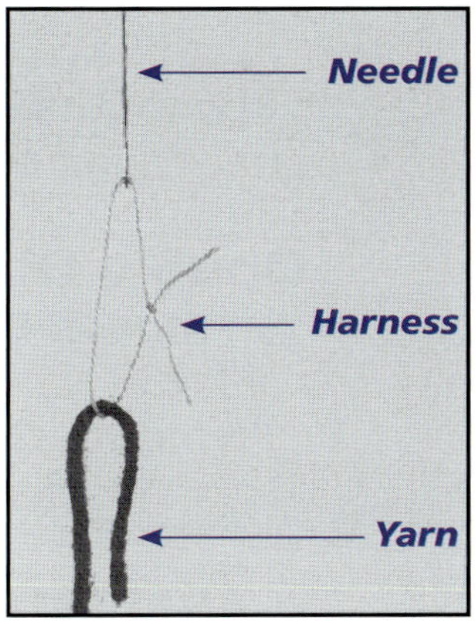

Using the tip of the needle, scoop up the beads, slide them down the needle and harness, and onto the yarn. String all the beads specified in the individual project instructions.

Hint: Do not use any beads that do not slide down easily over the eye of the needle.

Hint: When stringing beads, be sure the knot in the harness is at the side of the harness and not directly behind the eye of the needle or in the loop of the yarn.

Hint: To slip a bead(s), slide the bead(s) up the thread so that it rests between the last stitch knitted and the next stitch.

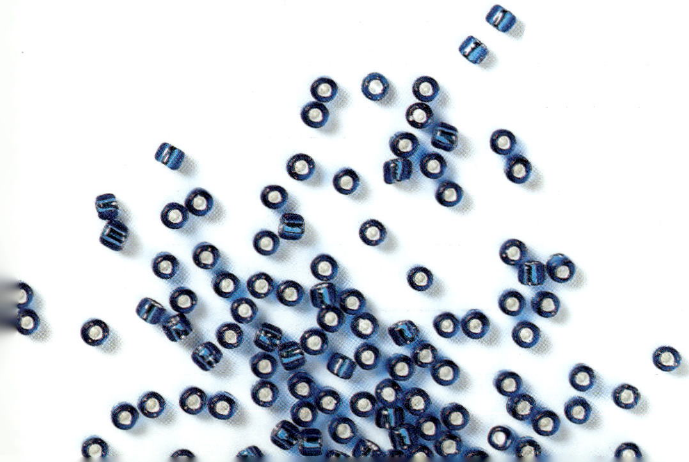

USING DOUBLE POINTED NEEDLES

When working too few stitches to use a circular needle, double pointed needles are required. Divide the stitches into thirds and slip one-third of the stitches onto each of 3 double pointed needles ***(Fig. 2)***, forming a triangle. With the fourth needle, knit across the stitches on the first needle ***(Fig. 3)***. You will now have an empty needle with which to knit the stitches from the next needle. Work the first stitch of each needle firmly to prevent gaps.

Fig. 2

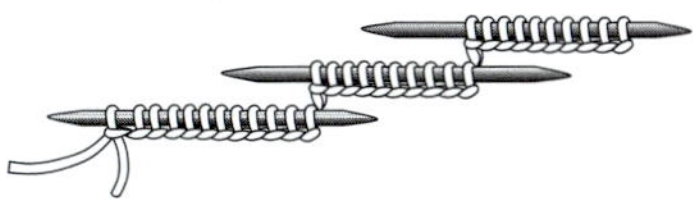

Fig. 3

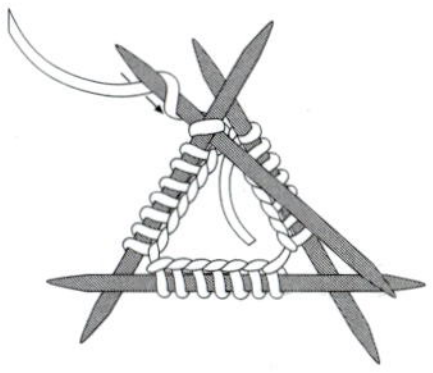

KNIT INCREASE

Knit the next stitch but do not slip, the old stitch off the left needle ***(Fig. 4a)***. Insert the right needle into the back loop of the same stitch and knit it ***(Fig. 4b)***, then slip the old stitch off the left needle.

Fig. 4a

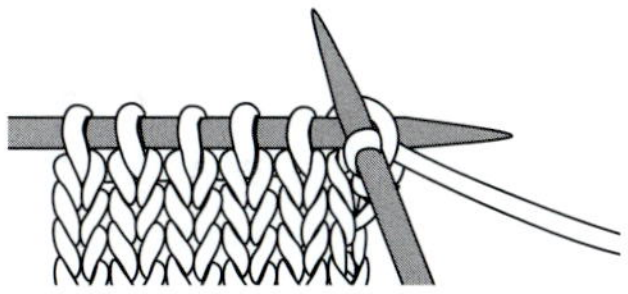

Fig. 4b

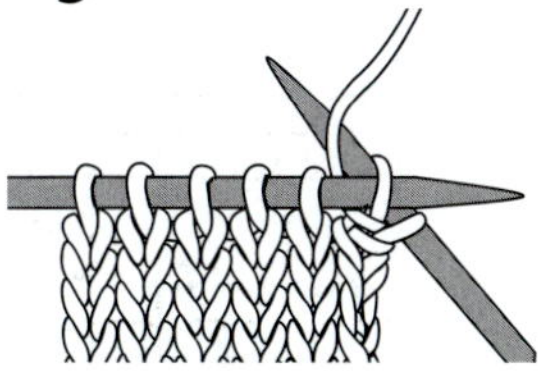

FINISHING

Cut yarn, leaving a 12" (30.5 cm) length for sewing. Thread needle with long end. Weave needle through remaining sts on last Rnd; leave end hanging and do **not** cut. Thread needle with long yarn end at cast on edge. Weave needle through sts at cast on edge; gather tightly. Sew seam then secure end.

Remove ornament cap. Slip ornament into body and pull yarn tail snug around neck of ornament. Wrap tail around neck approximately 5 times, cut excess yarn, place a dot of glue in two places and replace ornament cap.

Note: Any beads that may have slipped out of place can be returned to their proper place with the end of a needle or your fingers.

Yarn Information

All Ornaments in this leaflet were made using Sport Weight Yarn.
Any brand of Sport Weight Yarn may be used. Remember, to arrive at the finished size,
it is the GAUGE/TENSION that is most important, not the brand of yarn.
For your convenience, listed below are yarns used to create our photography models.

Christmas Joy
Bernat® Cool Crochet
#74242 Sage
Patons® Brilliant
#03023 Gold Glow
Plymouth Gold Rush
#40 Magenta

Windowpanes
Bernat® Cool Crochet
#74242 Sage
#74315 Amethyst
Plymouth Gold Rush
#36 Turquoise

Fleur De Lis
Bernat ®Cool Crochet
#74315 Amethyst
Patons® Brilliant
#03012 Earthy Glow
Plymouth Gold Rush
#46 Red

Ups and Downs
Patons® Brilliant
#04940 Black Dazzle
Plymouth Gold Rush
#43 Purple

Zig Zag
Bernat® Cool Crochet
#74430 Victorian
Patons Brilliant
#03232 Green Glitter
Plymouth Gold Rush
#10 White

Cross
Bernat® Cool Crochet
#74005 Crisp White
Plymouth Gold Rush
#4 Gold

Diamond
Patons® Brilliant
#03425 Sparkling Rose
Plymouth Gold Rush
205 Pastel Variegated

Vertical
Patons® Brilliant
#03416 Perfect Pastels
Plymouth Gold Rush
color number unavailable

Holiday Greetings
Patons® Brilliant
#04940 Black Dazzle
#03005 White Twinkle
Plymouth Gold Rush
color number unavailable

Double Diamonds
Patons® Brilliant
#03233 Natural Glow
Plymouth Gold Rush
color number unavailable

Diamond Trio
Bernat® Cool Crochet
#74435 Velveteen
Patons® Brilliant
#03008 Crystal Cream

Hearts
Bernat® Cool Crochet
#74005 Crisp White
Plymouth Gold Rush
#44 Green

Production Team:

Instructional Writer - Jean W. Lewis; **Technical Editor** - Lois J. Long; **Editorial Writer** - Susan McManus Johnson; **Senior Graphic Artist** - Chaska Richardson Lucas; **Graphic Artist** - Elaine Wheat; **Photo Stylist** - Sondra Daniel; and **Photographer** - Jerry Davis.

Projects made and instructions tested by Susan Carter, Sue Galucki, and Raymelle Greening.

We have made every effort to ensure that these instructions are accurate and complete. We cannot, however, be responsible for human error, typographical mistakes, or variations in individual work.

ISBN-13: 978-1-60140-370-4
ISBN-10: 1-60140-370-4